North York Moors

GW00646203

BRADWELL
BOOKS

A TASTE OF THE NORTH YORK MOORS

GREAT AYTON · BATTERSBY · ROBIN HOOD'S BAY · HELMSLEY

Introduction

Welcome to Bradwell's Images of the North York Moors – a lovingly prepared collection of photographs that cannot fail to whet your appetite to explore the region for yourself, and we hope will act as a constant reminder of the sheer beauty of the North York Moors.

Photographers Susan and Andrew Caffrey have a deep passion for the North York Moors and its delightful landscape, a passion that is clearly reflected in each of these unique and stunning images. The book is divided into twelve distinct areas, each with a short introductory paragraph outlining its main features; however, we think the photographs really speak for themselves.

Enjoy!

Whitby

Whitby is a classic seaside resort famous for its superb beaches and impressive pier. Its parks and gardens are home to an array of wildlife, and whale-watching is a favourite pastime. The imposing remains of Whitby Abbey, with over 2,000 years of history, form one of England's most important historical sites.

Whitby Abbey

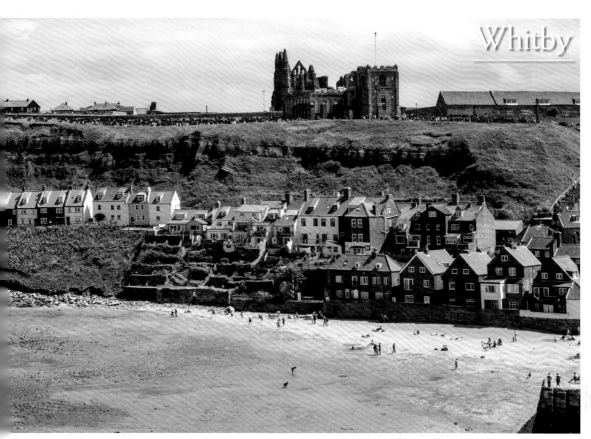

THE Hole OF Horcum

The story goes that this huge natural amphitheatre was created during an argument between a giant and his wife. One of the county's most spectacular sights, the Hole is best viewed from the A169 Pickering to Whitby road. Visitors can also follow Levisham Beck into the hollow itself.

Hutton LE Hole

The village of Hutton-le-Hole is known as one of the most picturesque in the area. Come to walk, cycle, or simply enjoy an ice cream on the green. The open-air Ryedale Folk Museum houses collections in historic buildings on rural local life from the Iron Age to the 1950s.

Great Ayton

The pretty village of Great Ayton sits on the banks of the River Leven. The village's ancient origins are evident in several Neolithic sites within the parish boundary. To the north, the iconic Roseberry Topping hill is in view – the summit can be reached via a gentle walk from the station.

Staithes

Staithes is a coastal hamlet in the borough of Scarborough and a favoured destination for fossil-hunting. With its winding streets and dramatic cliffs, Staithes is the quintessential fishing village. Boat trips give opportunities to fish and to see birds, dolphins and other marine life.

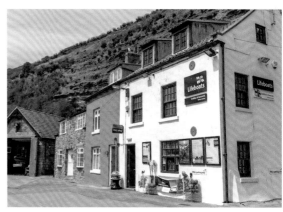

Thornton LE Dale

Traditional and picturesque, the village of Thornton-le-Dale offers thatched cottages, independent shops and a variety of local walks. Nearby Dalby Forest has plenty of opportunities for walking, cycling and wildlife-watching, and is also an excellent spot to see the night sky in free public stargazing sessions.

Lady Lumley's Alms Houses Founded in 1656

Helmsley

Helmsley is the only market town in the North York Moors and a popular base for exploring the wider area. The town itself offers unique attractions including Helmsley Castle, an arts centre and the Walled Gardens, as well as its own brewery and award-winning eateries.

Helmsley Castle established 1120/1130

Robin Hood's Bay

Robin Hood's Bay is the place to see Yorkshire's coastline at its most rugged, but you'll find sandy, family beaches here too. The village is home to many musicians and artists, and a huge variety of species inhabit the rock pools, cliff ledges and hedgerows.

Sutton Bank

The view of the Vale of York from atop Sutton Bank is renowned as one of the finest in England. There is a variety of walking and cycling trails to explore, while the visitor centre offers excellent birdwatching facilities. Look out for members of the Yorkshire Gliding Club soaring overhead.

Grosmont

The quiet village of Grosmont lies in the Esk Valley. Visitors can ride the North Yorkshire Moors Railway and see the world's oldest passenger railway tunnel. A popular walking trail starts in the village and traces the original railway line for 3½ miles to Goathland via Beck Hole.

THE Lord Stones

Lord Stones Country Park on Carlton Bank is a rambler's paradise, with three of the country's most popular trails: the Cleveland Way, the Lyke Wake Walk and the Coast to Coast. The stones themselves stand on a Bronze Age mound and are believed to have marked ancient land boundaries.

Commondale

The peaceful farming village of Commondale features 18th-century holiday cottages and a village pub. A pleasant short walk east to Castleton gives majestic views across the dale, while the nine-mile Moorland Magic walk is a longer but gentle trail over moorland and across fields.

A TASTE OF THE NORTH YORK MOORS

HELMSLEY • WHITBY • ROSEBERRY TOPPING • THE HOLE OF HORCUM